Burnet Hill Library
25 Byron Place
Livingston, N.J. 07

D0927915

# KAREEM ABDUL-JABBAR

## BASKETBALL GREAT
## BY
## JACOB MARGOLIES

**FRANKLIN WATTS**
New York ● London ● Toronto ● Sydney

A First Book

Cover photo copyright © Focus on Sports

Photographs copyright ©: NBA Photos/Andrew Bernstein: pp. 1, 55;
AP/Wide World Photos: pp. 8, 23, 30, 33, 35, 39, 43; UPI/Bettmann
Newsphotos: pp. 11, 14, 20, 31 bottom, 41, 47, 52; Naismith
Memorial Basketball Hall of Fame, Springfield, MA.: p. 17;
UCLA Department of Athletics: pp. 26, 31 top, 58;
Andy Hayt/Sports Illustrated: p. 49.

Library of Congress Cataloging-in-Publication Data

Margolies, Jacob.
Kareem Abdul-Jabbar : basketball great / by Jacob Margolies.
p. cm. — (A First book)
Includes bibliographical references (p.   ) and index.
Summary: Describes the life and basketball career of Kareem Abdul-
Jabbar.
ISBN 0-531-20076-0
1. Abdul-Jabbar, Kareem, 1947-   —Juvenile literature.
2. Basketball players—United States—Biography. [1. Abdul-Jabbar,
Kareem, 1947-  2. Basketball players.  3. Afro-Americans—
Biography.]  I. Title.  II. Series.
GV884.A24M37   1992
796.323′092—dc20
(B)                                                           91-31662 CIP AC

Copyright © 1992 by Jacob Margolies
All rights reserved
Printed in the United States of America
6  5  4  3  2

# CONTENTS

# INTRODUCING KAREEM
## ABDUL-JABBAR

The man wearing the gold jersey with number 33 on the back runs down the basketball court in long, graceful strides. As he nears the basket, he reaches out his long arms and calls for the ball. When he gets it, he turns quickly, and with his right hand stretching high over his head, he releases the ball with a final snap of his wrist. The ball rises in a high arc and then drops straight through the net. Over 17,000 fans in the Los Angeles Forum roar their approval.

The player who has made this beautiful shot—the "skyhook"—is a giant of a man. He is 7 feet 2 inches (2.5 m) tall, and weighs over 260 pounds (118 kg). His head is shaved and he is wearing goggles to protect his eyes. His distinctive appearance is known to basketball fans throughout the world.

Playing until the age of forty-two, this man is, as he ends his career in 1989, many years older than any other player in the National Basketball Association. His team, the Los Angeles Lakers, has been world champion five times during the 1980s. Kareem-Abdul Jabbar is the man's name, and many people believe that he is the greatest basketball player of all time.

# GROWING UP

**1**

Kareem Abdul-Jabbar was born in New York on April 16, 1947 and named Ferdinand Lewis Alcindor, Jr. He changed his name to Kareem Abdul-Jabbar in 1971 for religious reasons after he became a Muslim. Until that time, Kareem was known as Lew Alcindor.

Lew Alcindor grew up in the neighborhood of Inwood in New York City. Inwood was then, and still is, largely a neighborhood of immigrants—people who have recently arrived in the United States from other countries. In the housing project where Lew grew up, he knew people from China, Russia, Cuba, the Dominican Republic, the Philippines, and the West Indies.

As the only child of Ferdinand and Cora

Alcindor, Lew received a lot of attention. Ferdinand Alcindor worked as a police officer for the New York City Housing Authority and for the Transit Authority. He was also a jazz musician and a graduate of the famous Juilliard School of Music. Cora Alcindor took care of the household. Education was considered very important in the Alcindor home. Lew's parents sent him to a Catholic elementary school in the neighborhood, St. Jude's.

Even as a young boy Lew Alcindor was extremely tall for his age. At the age of nine, Lew was already 5 feet 8 inches (1.73 m) tall. He grew so quickly that for a while he was awkward and uncoordinated. Lew played on St. Jude's basketball team in the fifth and sixth grades. Although he was the tallest member of the team, he seldom got to actually play in the games. When he got the ball, he often fumbled or dropped it, and other kids made fun of his exceptional height. Older boys in the neighborhood sometimes started fights with Lew.

*The fabulous number 33*
*in action for the*
*Los Angeles Lakers*

Lew Alcindor kept practicing, and by the time he was in the eighth grade he had become an excellent player. One day when he was thirteen and playing in an eighth-grade game, Lew caught a pass and "dunked" the basketball for the first time in his life. In a dunk shot, a player takes the ball, leaps above the basket, and stuffs the ball through the hoop. Lew's teammates and coaches were amazed, and Lew was excited, too, at making such a spectacular shot. It was a moment he would remember all his life.

By the time he was ready to graduate from the eighth grade, basketball coaches from high schools all over New York City were trying to convince Lew Alcindor to come to their schools. Lew and his parents decided he whould go to Power Memorial High School, a private Catholic school.

##  HIGH SCHOOL YEARS

Basketball at Power Memorial was serious business. From the start, Lew Alcindor was playing

*Lew Alcindor playing for Power Memorial High School in a championship game at Madison Square Garden*

with and against some of the best high school players in the United States. Lew was playing several hours every day and was constantly improving. By the time he was in the tenth grade, Lew Alcindor was the star center at Power Memorial. The team won the New York City Catholic High School Championship, and newspapers all over the country started writing about the 6-foot 11-inch (2.11 m) Alcindor.

During the summers of his high school years, Alcindor played basketball on the playgrounds of Harlem. Harlem is a historic Manhattan neighborhood just south of Inwood, and is a center of African-American life in New York City. When he was fifteen, Lew met Wilt Chamberlain—the greatest basketball player of the time. Chamberlain, who was playing in a summer league in Harlem, was bigger, stronger, and more graceful than any other big man playing basketball. Even though Chamberlain was ten years older than Lew, the two seven-footers saw a lot of each other over the summer. Both Chamberlain and Alcindor loved jazz and they often went to hear musicians play in different parts of the city.

As his basketball skills continued to improve, Alcindor was learning and maturing off the court as well. During the summer of 1964, Alcindor worked as a reporter for a weekly newspaper put out by the Harlem Youth Project, a city-funded summer program. He covered events such as the New York visit of the civil rights leader Dr. Martin Luther King, Jr. Alcindor also began studying the history of the Harlem Renaissance, a period during the 1920s when many great African-American writers and artists lived and worked in Harlem. Through his studies, Alcindor learned about the history and accomplishments of African Americans. Later that summer, when angry racial protests broke out in Harlem, young Alcindor covered those troubled days as a reporter. Though Lew Alcindor played basketball against some of the greatest playground players in the world that summer, he remembers the lessons he learned off the court as more important in his development.

During Alcindor's final two years of high school, Power Memorial had the best team in the United States. By the time he finished high school in 1965, college coaches from all over the country were trying to convince the Alcindor family that Lew should attend their college. Lew had worked hard in his classes and was an excellent student, so he had the opportunity to go anywhere he wanted. Even Harvard, one of the most

academically demanding universities in the United States, was anxious to have Alcindor. Choosing which college to attend was a very difficult decision for Lew Alcindor.

*Lew Alcindor proudly displays his Most Valuable Player trophy, presented to him while he was playing for Power Memorial High School.*

# ABOUT

## BASKETBALL

**2**

Before continuing Lew Alcindor's story, let's take a closer look at the sport of basketball. The game that he loved and that made him famous has an interesting history.

In 1892, Dr. James Naismith was a physical education teacher at the YMCA in Springfield, Massachusetts. Dr. Naismith wanted to find a game or activity to keep his students busy between football in the fall and baseball in the spring. Because the winter was very cold in Massachusetts, the students' recreation activities had to be indoors. At first Dr. Naismith tried to have the students play outdoor games, such as soccer,

*Dr. James Naismith,*
*the man who invented*
*the sport of basketball,*
*posing for an unusual*
*basketball shot: attempting*
*to score by shooting*
*below his waist and*
*into a peach basket*

in the gym. But these outdoor sports were unsuitable for the smaller space of a gym. Students sometimes broke windows or were injured.

Then Naismith had an idea. He asked the janitor of the building to hang peach baskets from the balconies at each end of the gym. The baskets were 10 feet (3.04 m) above the gym floor. Then he got a large ball, and divided his students into two teams. He made up thirteen rules. The main rule was that players could not run with the ball. The object of the game was for each team to shoot the ball into its own basket, and to prevent the other team from scoring baskets. Dr. Naismith told his students that this was his last attempt to find a new game to be played in the gym. If they didn't like this game he had invented, he would give up. Dr. Naismith didn't need to worry. His students loved the game, and basketball was born.

## ● THE BASKETBALL GAME ●

Today basketball and soccer are the two most popular team sports in the world. Basketball can be played indoors or outdoors. In an official basketball game, each team has five members, and the teams shoot at baskets on opposite ends of the court. It is possible, though, to play with only two, four, or six people, and using only one basket, if there are not enough people or space for a regulation-style game.

A five-person team is made up of a center, two forwards, and two guards. Kareem Abdul-Jabbar played as a center. The center is usually the tallest player on the team. On offense, the center stays close to the basket. That way he or she can receive a pass from one of the other players and be ready to take a shot; or if another player shoots and misses, the center will be in position to rebound the missed shot. To rebound means to recover or retrieve a missed shot.

On defense, the center usually guards the opposing team's center. Also, the center tries to be in position to get defensive rebounds and to block shots taken by the opposing team. Kareem Abdul-Jabbar was known as a great scorer, but he was also an excellent rebounder and shot blocker. Until recently, the center was the dominant position in basketball. For a team to win, it needed a center who was very talented. In recent years though, teams without a great center have been successful. Although the center is still important, teams that do not have a star center can win by stressing speed, defense, and accurate shooting.

The two guards generally do most of the dribbling and passing. The team with the ball tries to move the ball closer to the basket by either passing or dribbling. A player dribbles the ball by bouncing it with one hand. A player with the ball cannot take more than two steps without dribbling. Often one guard will be an excellent shooter, while the other will be more responsible for passing and directing the team. The guards are usually the quickest and shortest players on the team.

The two forwards are responsible for rebounding and scoring. They move back and forth from very near the basket—the area where the center usually is—to farther away from the basket. On defense, the guards and forwards will usually guard the opposing players who play their same positions.

A player can score two types of baskets. A basket scored in the flow of the game is a field goal and is usually worth 2 points. Kareem

*Lew Alcindor shows students in Long Island City how to hold the ball for a dunk shot.*

Abdul-Jabbar scored more field goals than any other player in the history of professional basketball. Wilt Chamberlain scored the second highest number of field goals. If a player makes a shot from behind the 3-point line —nearly 20 feet (6 m) from the basket in high school and college games—that field goal is worth 3 points. Three-point shots are rare because it is hard to score a basket from so far away.

The second type of basket is the free throw. A player gets to take a free throw—an unguarded shot at the basket—when the player is fouled by a defender. A foul is called if a player bumps, pushes, holds, trips, or hits an opposing player. The fouled player can then shoot a free throw from directly behind the free-throw line, 15 feet (4.57 m) from the basket. A free throw is worth 1 point.

These are some of the basic rules of basketball. The best way to learn the rules, though, is to play the game. Basketball is fun and good exercise, too. You don't need fancy or expensive equipment to play. All you need is a basketball and a basket. There is probably a playground near your house with a basketball court. Some families have basketball hoops in their driveways; also, school yards, Y's and sports clubs usually have courts.

*Auburn plays Louisiana Tech during the Women's NCAA Final Four Tournament.*

*Kareem's last exhibition game. He led the American all-star team to a 133–117 victory over the Taiwan team.*

Boys and girls of all ages play basketball. Women's basketball is popular at colleges and schools across the country. Basketball has also become an international sport, played in countries throughout the world. The player who replaced Kareem Abdul-Jabbar as the center for the Los Angeles Lakers is from Yugoslavia. His name is Vlade Divac. The National Basketball Association (NBA), the top professional league in the United States, has players from Nigeria, the Sudan, Germany, and the Soviet Union.

In the 1988 Olympic Games, the men's basketball team from the Soviet Union beat the American team and won the gold medal. The Olympic Game rules did not allow any American professional players to play, so only college players from the United States competed. The Olympic rules have been changed so that now the best American players will be able to play in the Olympic Games.

When Kareem Abdul-Jabbar retired after the 1989 season, he took a final playing tour abroad with a group of NBA players. They played in Australia and Taiwan. Basketball today is a sport loved all over the world.

# LEW ALCINDOR

## GOES TO COLLEGE

As Lew Alcindor finished his terrific high school basketball career at Power Memorial, he narrowed his choice of colleges down to four—Columbia University and St. John's in New York, the University of Michigan, and UCLA, the University of California at Los Angeles.

Lew went out to visit the UCLA campus and was very impressed. The campus was beautiful, the school had a good academic reputation, and the basketball team was the defending college champion.

One of Lew's heroes, Jackie Robinson, had attended UCLA many years earlier. Robinson joined the Brooklyn Dodgers baseball team in 1947, becoming the first African-American to

*The UCLA athletics department*

play major league baseball. Alcindor's African-American heritage was important to him, and the fact that Robinson, an earlier African-American sports hero, had attended UCLA might have influenced him.

What finally convinced Lew Alcindor to attend UCLA was the school's coach, John Wooden. Wooden and Alcindor seemed like two very different people. Wooden was a middle-aged white man who had been brought up in a small town in the Midwest, and Alcindor was young, black, and from New York City. Actually, Alcindor found a lot about Coach Wooden that made him feel comfortable. Both Wooden and Alcindor were quiet, calm, and very determined. Alcindor felt Wooden really cared about his players. Also, Wooden had great knowledge of the game of basketball, and Lew knew that he could learn a lot about the game playing for UCLA.

When Lew Alcindor went to college, first-year students were not allowed to play on the varsity college level. There was a separate freshman team. The idea behind this was to allow new students to get used to college life before they became involved in time-consuming varsity sports.

The UCLA freshman team of 1965–66 practiced hard. Alcindor learned different practice drills that improved his stamina. The freshman team won all the games it played that year. They even beat the UCLA varsity team in a practice game. Everyone was excited about the following year, when Alcindor and some of his teammates would play on the varsity team.

The UCLA 1966–67 basketball squad was a great team. Alcindor was already, in the opinion of most observers, the best center in college basketball. The team had some other excellent college players, especially the guards Lucius Allen and Mike Warren. All year UCLA did not lose a game. In the year-end National Collegiate Athletic Association (NCAA) Tournament, UCLA met the University of Houston in the semifinals. Houston's center, Elvin Hayes, was a great shooter and rebounder. Hayes predicted before the game that his team would beat UCLA. In the game, Hayes outscored Alcindor, but UCLA still won by 15 points. UCLA easily defeated Dayton University in the championship game. Lew was elated. He had led his team to the NCAA 1966–67 championship!

# ● ALCINDOR AND ELVIN HAYES ●
## MEET AGAIN

The next year would pose new challenges for the UCLA team. During the off-season, the college rules had been changed to outlaw the dunk. Many people thought the new rule was specifically aimed to try to limit Alcindor's dominance in the college game. It did not work. As the season progressed, the UCLA team continued to beat everyone.

Then in a game against the University of California, Alcindor was accidentally scratched on his left eyeball by a California player. The pain was terrible and Alcindor couldn't see out of the eye. He was taken to the hospital, and then wore a patch over his left eye for three days.

Eight days after his injury, UCLA was scheduled to play Houston. Elvin Hayes had been saying that he thought Alcindor was an overrated player. The game was played in the Houston Astrodome before the biggest crowd ever to see a college basketball game. There were over 52,000 people in the Astrodome, and sportswriters called the game the biggest basketball game ever. Alcindor still could not see very well but he wanted to play, and Coach Wooden de-

*Above: In this three-way photo,
Lew Alcindor easily keeps the ball,
then brings his long arm far back,
to finally pass the ball to a teammate on the UCLA team.
Facing page top: The 1967 UCLA team.
Lew Alcindor is easy to spot.
Facing page bottom: UCLA
winning the NCAA title in 1967*

cided to let him try. It was a big mistake. Hayes played magnificently, and Lew had the worst game of his college career. Houston won by 2 points.

Afterward, newspapers all over the country criticized Alcindor's performance. Hayes was named College Player of the Year largely because of his play in the UCLA game. Few people seemed to remember that Alcindor had been playing with a serious injury. The criticism by the press made Alcindor angry. But the season was not over, and the UCLA team was determined to avenge their loss.

Lew's eye healed. Neither UCLA nor Houston lost another game the rest of the year. During the end-of-the-season NCAA tournament, UCLA and Houston would once again face off against each other. Basketball fans everywhere awaited the rematch eagerly. This time Alcindor and UCLA were ready. The entire team was making its shots, and Hayes found it very difficult to score against the tight UCLA defense. The nightmare of Lew's poor game at the Astrodome inspired him in this game. UCLA demolished Houston by 32 points.

In the 1968 tournament final, UCLA easily beat North Carolina. UCLA was the college basketball champion again, and for the second

*Lew Alcindor practicing with his
injured eye before the Houston
game in the Astrodome*

straight year Alcindor was named the tournament's Most Valuable Player.

## ● SUMMING UP THE COLLEGE YEARS ●

During his final year at UCLA (1968–69), Alcindor had to adjust to some new players. Once again, however, the UCLA team was the best in the country. The team lost only one game all year, and again they won the NCAA championship tournament. During Alcindor's years at UCLA, the college became the first team ever to win three straight national championships.

Lew graduated from UCLA in four years. Besides becoming the best college basketball player of his day, he had also gotten a solid education.

During his college years, Alcindor had begun to study the religion of Islam. Lew admired and had been influenced by the African-American Muslim leader Malcolm X during the summer of 1964. During his summers in New York, between college years at UCLA, Alcindor devoted himself to learning about Islam. He read the Koran, the holy book of Islam, and learned about the laws and rituals that Muslims

*The African-American Muslim leader Malcolm X
speaks before a huge crowd in Harlem.*

follow. Eventually he came to consider himself a Muslim. Although he did not tell many people, Alcindor took the name of Kareem Abdul-Jabbar as his Muslim name. It would be several years, however, before Alcindor would legally change his name.

During his days at UCLA, Lew also became friends with the famous movie star and martial arts master Bruce Lee, who taught him kung fu, the Chinese art of self-defense. Alcindor found the discipline and intense concentration it required were skills that he could use on the basketball court.

Of the many people who influenced him during college, Kareem today remembers Coach John Wooden as the most important. Speaking of those years, Kareem Abdul-Jabbar says, "Coach Wooden had faith in us as players and human beings, and he was a great teacher. My relationship with him has been one of the most significant of my life."

# LEW TURNS PRO

## 4

Lew Alcindor was now ready to become a professional basketball player. He was the first college player to be drafted in 1969, by both the Milwaukee Bucks in the NBA and the New York Nets of the American Basketball Association, a rival league that no longer exists. The two teams were desperate to have him, and Alcindor was faced with a difficult decision. The Bucks played in the more established NBA, but Alcindor was eager to return to New York.

Lew and his advisors told the teams that they could each make only one contract offer. The Bucks offered Lew a five-year contract. The New York Nets' offer was for a lot less money. The next day the Nets team tried to make a new offer but Alcindor felt that this went against the rules he had set up. Although he had hoped to play in New York, Alcindor would be playing in Milwaukee. Thanks to his big contract, he was now a rich man.

As Alcindor began his professional career, there was some question about whether he would still be able to dominate the game as he had in college. Professional basketball is much rougher and more physical than the college game. Sportswriters wondered if Alcindor's graceful game could withstand the elbowing, pushing, and holding of seasoned professional players.

Lew's relationship with the media at this time was strained. Many reporters thought he was moody and impolite. Actually, once a writer gained Alcindor's trust, there was no problem. Because Lew thought he had been treated unfairly by reporters, however, he was suspicious of the press.

Lew quickly removed any doubts people had about his ability to star at the highest level. Milwaukee had been the worst team in the league, and Alcindor turned them around almost by himself. He averaged nearly 30 points a game in his first year, and was chosen as the NBA's Rookie of the Year. Alcindor was often

*Lew Alcindor puts his signature
on a professional basketball contract
with the Milwaukee Bucks.*

guarded by two defenders, and when this happened he would make a pass to his open teammate who would usually score an easy basket. The Bucks lost to the New York Knicks in the playoffs in 1969–70, but they had improved tremendously.

The next year the Bucks added Oscar Robertson to their team. Nicknamed "the Big O," many people believe that Robertson is the best guard who ever played basketball. He was a great scorer, passer, and rebounder, and at 6 feet 5 inches (1.9 m) and 210 pounds (95 kg), he was extremely big and strong for a guard. Robertson was thirty-two years old and nearing the end of his career, but his addition to the Bucks immediately made them an excellent team.

Alcindor was very excited about playing with Robertson. Now Lew had someone who could always find ways to pass the ball to him in

*Wilt Chamberlain of the Los Angeles Lakers, Kareem Abdul-Jabbar of the Milwaukee Bucks, Jerry West of the Lakers, and Oscar Robertson of the Bucks (left to right) go for a loose ball during this game.*

a position where he could then score. Robertson was great at passing off for assists. A player is credited with an assist when his pass to a teammate directly results in a basket.

It was quite a year. The Bucks were now a top team and, for the first time, Alcindor got to go up against his childhood hero Wilt Chamberlain. Chamberlain, who was playing for the Los Angeles Lakers, had been injured and unable to play during Lew's rookie season.

Alcindor held his own against Wilt. Chamberlain was used to being the top center in the game and he may have been jealous of all the attention Alcindor was receiving. After he joined the National Basketball Association, Alcindor was never again friendly with Chamberlain.

The Bucks won the NBA Championship in the 1970–71 season, and Alcindor was named the league's Most Valuable Player. Many great players are on teams that never win an NBA Championship, and it would be many years before Alcindor would again be on a championship team.

After the 1970–71 season, Alcindor legally changed his name to Kareem Abdul-Jabbar. While Alcindor had become a Muslim several years earlier, he now felt the time was right to

*Kareem Abdul-Jabbar makes his name
change official, preferring to be
known by his Islamic name.*

publicly take a new name to indicate his religious beliefs.

During his years playing for Milwaukee, Kareem married. Kareem and his wife had three children together, but the marriage was not a happy one and did not last. Later in his career, Kareem had a fourth child with another woman. Kareem's children have always been an important part of his life.

Kareem Abdul-Jabbar played for four more years for the Milwaukee Bucks. During those years the Bucks had some very good teams, but they never managed to win the NBA Championship again.

In 1974, the Bucks came very close to winning it all. They played the Boston Celtics in the finals. In the sixth game, the Celtics were winning by one point with only a few seconds left in the game when Kareem shot a beautiful skyhook shot that swished through the net to win the game. In the final game, though, the Celtics were victorious, winning the exciting series four games to three. That year Kareem was voted the Most Valuable Player for a third time, but he was still unhappy. Kareem Abdul-Jabbar has always been far more interested in seeing his team win than in any accomplishments he might achieve as an individual.

The next year was even worse. Oscar Robertson had retired and the Milwaukee team, with the exception of Kareem, was not very good. Kareem missed six weeks of the season with a broken hand. The Bucks finished the 1974–75 season in last place. It was Kareem's first losing season since he had been a twelve-year-old at St. Jude's.

Kareem Abdul-Jabbar was ready for a change in his life. He asked to be traded. The Bucks agreed to his request, and after the 1975 season, he was traded to the Los Angeles Lakers. Abdul-Jabbar would be returning to the city of his college days! After the cold winters of Milwaukee, he was excited about going back to the West Coast.

# THE LAKER YEARS
## AND AFTER

5

Like the Bucks, the Lakers were not a very good team when Kareem first joined them. Although they won more games than they lost, they were still not ready to win the NBA championship. Abdul-Jabbar was once again voted the Most Valuable Player in 1976 and 1977, but he had little help from his teammates.

After being poked in the eyes several times and suffering some serious eye injuries, Abdul-Jabbar had started wearing large protective goggles during his final year in Milwaukee. In Los Angeles, he continued wearing them. Although it looked a little strange, people got used to it. The goggles became part of Kareem's unique and distinctive look. In later years, a few other players also started wearing goggles.

*Kareem Abdul-Jabbar wears*
*protective goggles for the first*
*time in a game, a practice he was*
*to continue throughout his career.*

Life with the Los Angeles Lakers changed in 1980 when Earvin "Magic" Johnson left college and joined the team. Magic was an energetic and exciting guard who passed the ball beautifully. Standing 6 feet 9 inches (2.1 m), he was much taller than any player at his position. Magic could score and rebound when necessary. What Magic loved more than anything else, however, was passing the basketball to teammates in positions where they could score easily.

At last Kareem Abdul-Jabbar had a teammate who could help him make the Los Angeles Lakers the best in the world of basketball. Kareem knew he had been lucky to play with Oscar Robertson in Milwaukee. Now, he would have a chance to play with another great playmaking guard.

Kareem is twelve years older than Magic Johnson and, partly because of the difference in their ages, it took some time before the two players became close friends. Kareem and Magic have different personalities on the basketball court. Abdul-Jabbar is serious and usually does

*The incredible team*
*of Magic Johnson (right)*
*and Kareem Abdul-Jabbar (left)*

not show his emotions. Magic Johnson, on the other hand, is very outgoing when he plays. Often after the Lakers score a dramatic basket, Magic will hug and embrace his teammates. In spite of these differences, Kareem's and Magic's styles of play worked well together. Both men were intelligent, unselfish, and determined to win.

In 1980, Magic's first year with Los Angeles, the Lakers reached the NBA championship. Kareem had not been on a championship team in nine years and he really wanted to win. The Lakers were playing the Philadelphia 76ers. In the fifth game, with the series tied at two games apiece, Kareem sprained his ankle. He kept playing despite being in a lot of pain, and scored 40 points to lead his team to victory. Afterward he could hardly walk. In the sixth game of the series, Kareem was not able to play, but the Lakers, led by a great effort from Magic Johnson, won anyway.

The Lakers were champions and Kareem was named the season's Most Valuable Player for a sixth time. No other player has won this award so many times, and this was the last time in his career that Kareem would win it.

The Lakers were now the best team in basketball. Their opponents knew that to be considered a top team, they would have to beat Los Angeles. In 1982 the Lakers, led by Kareem and Magic, were again world champions. Kareem was hoping his team could repeat as champions the next year.

In the middle of the 1982–83 season, Kareem Abdul-Jabbar had a very unhappy experience. His house burned down in a fire. Everything that Kareem had collected over the years was destroyed. Fortunately, nobody was hurt. Abdul-Jabbar was upset, but he was moved by the kindness of many people who sent him notes and gifts. Kareem tried to concentrate on basketball. The Lakers got to the championship round, but many of their players were injured and they lost to Philadelphia.

The next year, the 1983–84 season, was special for Kareem because he broke Wilt Chamberlain's career scoring record of 34,419 points. As the Lakers traveled around the country, fans flocked to games hoping to see Abdul-Jabbar break the record. The basket that made Kareem the all-time scoring leader came on April 5, 1984 against the Utah Jazz. It seemed right that the basket that broke the record was a skyhook— the shot for which Kareem will always be remembered.

The playoffs turned out to be a bitter disap-

*Kareem Abdul-Jabbar holds up
the NBA World Championship Trophy
after the Los Angeles Lakers won it
by beating the Philadelphia 76ers
with a score of 114–104.*

pointment. Los Angeles played the Boston Celtics. The Celtics and Lakers were the two best teams of the 1980s, but they had not played against each other in a championship series in many years. Kareem remembered losing a championship to Boston in seven games when he had played for Milwaukee, but this year he thought the Lakers could beat the Celtics. The series was tied at three games apiece. In the final game Boston, playing before their home fans and led by their star, Larry Bird, beat the Lakers. It was a close game. Kareem and his teammates thought they should have won. Despite becoming the highest scorer ever, Abdul-Jabbar felt disappointed as the series ended.

The Lakers and the Celtics got a chance to play each other for the championship again in 1985. Over their history, Boston had played Los Angeles seven times in the NBA finals, and every time Boston had won. In the first game of the series, Boston destroyed the Lakers 148 to 114. Nearly everyone figured that Los Angeles just could not beat Larry Bird's Celtic team. Kareem, Magic, and James Worthy, the Lakers' star forward, were determined not to give up. The next game was at Boston, and the noisy Celtic fans were stunned when the Lakers played brilliantly and won. Leading three games to two, the Lakers won the final game at Boston, 111 to 100. Kareem Abdul-Jabbar was thirty-eight years old and the Lakers were world champions. Kareem later said, "Beating Boston in 1985 is my greatest basketball moment. The victory brought the entire city of Los Angeles together. Boston had never before lost a seventh and deciding game in the championship round on their home court. It is something I will always remember."

Many people thought that Kareem Abdul-Jabbar would retire after 1985. He was older than any other person playing the game, and it seemed he had accomplished everything that a player could. But Kareem still loved the game and he was still one of the top centers in the league. He decided he was not ready to stop playing. In fact, Kareem would play for four more years!

In 1987, the Lakers once again beat the Boston Celtics to win the NBA Championship. Although he was not quite the dominant player he

*Beating the Boston Celtics again, Kareem and the Lakers win another championship.*

had been in his younger years, Abdul-Jabbar was still very good. Especially in the important games, Kareem was able to lead his team even though he was playing against people who were much younger than he.

No team had won the NBA Championship for two consecutive years since Boston in 1967 and 1968. There are so many good teams, and a season is so long and tiring that to repeat as a champion is extremely difficult. After winning in 1987, the Lakers were hoping to make history. The Lakers reached the 1988 Finals and faced a new opponent, the Detroit Pistons. Detroit was a younger team. They were very rough and physical, and they had great guards.

In game six of the series, it looked as if Detroit was about to become the new champion. Detroit was leading the series three games to two, and with only a few seconds left in the game, Detroit was ahead, 102 to 101. Then Kareem was fouled. He would shoot two free throws. After playing for nineteen years as a professional, Kareem knew he should concentrate and stay calm. Kareem made both free throws, and the Lakers won the game. Then they won the seventh and final game. The Lakers had repeated as champions. Basketball history had been made.

The next year, 1988–89, was Abdul-Jabbar's final year as a player. Every city in which the Lakers played had a special ceremony honoring Kareem for his great career and thanking him for all that he had given to basketball. The Boston Celtics gave Kareem a piece of the famous Boston Garden floor. His teammates gave him a Rolls Royce automobile. Everywhere he went fans and players thanked Kareem for the many happy memories he had given them through his long career.

All the players Kareem had played with when he first came into the league had retired many years earlier. Kareem Abdul-Jabbar played so well and for so long that he will always be an important part of the history of basketball.

During his final year, the Lakers again reached the NBA finals and again played Detroit. This time Detroit won. A new chapter was starting in basketball and Kareem Abdul-Jabbar's career was over.

Many people consider Kareem Abdul-Jabbar the greatest basketball player in the history of the game. He holds an astonishing number of records. During his college and professional career, he played on nine championship teams. He scored more points, blocked

more shots, and played more games than any player in the history of the NBA.

Since his retirement, Kareem has stayed active. He is interested in acting and has appeared on several television shows. Abdul-Jabbar now divides his time between Los Angeles and Hawaii. He is pleased that he now has lots of time to spend with his four children. Recently Abdul-Jabbar was honored at UCLA for his great college career. Although he has left the game, basketball fans will remember Kareem Abdul-Jabbar for a long time.

*UCLA retires
Kareem Abdul-Jabbar's
number 33 jersey.*

# GLOSSARY

**Assist**—a pass to a teammate that results directly in the teammate scoring a basket.

**Dribble**—to bounce the basketball continuously with one hand.

**Dunk**—a shot in which the player jumps above the basket and stuffs the ball through the hoop.

**Field goal**—a basket scored in the flow of the game.

**Foul**—illegal physical contact with an opposing player. Holding, grabbing, pushing, elbowing, and hitting are all examples of fouls.

**Free throw**—a shot that a player gets to take unguarded from the free throw line after he or she has been fouled. A made free throw is worth 1 point.

**Rebound**—to recover a missed shot that has bounced off the backboard or rim.

# FOR FURTHER
## READING

Antonacci, Robert J., and Jene Barr. *Basketball for Young Champions*. New York: McGraw-Hill, 1979.

Deuker, Carl. *On the Devil's Court*. New York: Little Brown, 1988 (fiction).

Frommer, Harvey. *Jackie Robinson*. New York: Franklin Watts, 1984.

Johnson, Earvin "Magic" and Roy S. Johnson. *Magic's Touch*. Boston: Addison-Wesley, 1989.

Laklan, Carli. *Golden Girls: True Stories of Olympic Women Stars*. New York: McGraw-Hill, 1980.

Newman, Matthew, and Dr. Harold Schroeder, eds. *Larry Bird*. Mankato, Minn.: Crestwood House, 1986.

# INDEX